MW00943091

In*card*ceration:
A collection of inspirational poems for the incarcerated community.

by Beverly Morgan

outskirts press

Denver, Colorado

Outskirts Press, Inc.
http://www.outskirtspress.com

ISBN: 978-1-4327-6629-0

Outskirts Press and the "OP" logo are trademarks belonging to Outskirts Press, Inc.

PRINTED IN THE UNITED STATES OF AMERICA

CONTENTS

TIME DOES NOT STAND STILL   1

HONESTY   2

LOVE   3

MISSING YOU   4

FOR THE GOOD TIMES   5

FATHER'S DAY   6

STAYING IN TOUCH   7

WE TRIED ALL WE COULD   8

BIRTH OF A CHILD   9

HAPPY BIRTHDAY MOTHER   10

HOLD ON TO GOD'S GRACE   11

LOYALTY   12

NEED OF A FRIEND   13

MERRY CHRISTMAS FATHER   14

MERRY CHRISTMAS MOTHER   15

HAPPY BIRTHDAY FATHER   16

REMEMBERING THE GOOD TIMES   17

FRIENDS FOR LIFE   18

KEEP YOUR HEAD UP   19

ENCOURAGEMENT   20

HANG TIGHT   21

WEDDING ANNIVERSARY   22

WE ARE IN THIS TOGETHER   23

MOTHER'S DAY   24

LOVE FOREVER   25

MISSING YOU   26

THOUGHTS OF FATHER 27

MOTHER PASSED 28

YOUR DNA WILL SOON SET YOU FREE 29

THE CIRCLE IS BROKEN 30

$$ TIME 31

FINDING HUMOR WHILE DOING TIME 32

THINK LIFE OVER
WHILE YOU'RE LOCKED AWAY 33

ENCOURAGEMENT FOR A PAROLE VIOLATOR 34

WE LOVE YOU UNCONDITIONALLY 35

YOUR INNOCENCE YOU MUST DEFEND
TO THE END 36

THE POLITICS OF PRISON LIFE 37

YOU WERE UNFAIRLY TREATED 38

THE POLITRICKS OF IMPRISONMENT 39

THE SYSTEM NEEDS MENDING 40

HEALING 41

GOD IS YOUR JUDGE 42

DISPENSATION OF JUSTICE, IS IT FOR REAL? 43

MISSING YOU AT THANKSGIVING 44

YOUR CHILDREN MISS YOU 45

YOUR DAUGHTER MISSES YOU 46

THE KIDS AND I MISS YOU A LOT 47

MISSING OUT ON FAMILY TIME 48

KEEPING IN TOUCH 49

GET OUT ALIVE 50

YOUR FAMILY'S THOUGHTS 51

THINK ON THESE THINGS... 52

DON'T BE DISMAYED 53

HAPPY VALENTINE'S DAY
TO MY LOVE DOING TIME   54
KEEPING YOU HAPPY   55
NEEDLESS PUNISHMENT   56
CHANGE YOUR POSTURE
WHILE YOU'RE DOING TIME   57
CELL BLOCK LIFE   58
TAKE HEED   59
TIME IN THE SERVICE
NOW TIME BEHIND BARS   60
PLAYING IT SAFE AND STAYING ALIVE   61

TIME DOES NOT STAND STILL

Don't blame the system
Don't blame the cops
Don't blame mother
Don't blame pops

Frankly speaking, you have got one person to blame
I hate pointing fingers as it always brings shame

There are situations in life that we cannot change
Consider them life's music, a little out of range

The bars of jail may not deliver
The tune you want to hear
Consider yourself an audience member
Who's just there to grin and bear

HONESTY

There is so much injustice and so many flaws
We tend to blame society's laws

Deplorable conditions must make you upset
But with a permanent smile… that you can offset

'Twas like a minute ago, everything seemed alright
I know you must ponder how you got in this plight

In spite of your discontent
If you are honest with self, the less you will lament

LOVE

Some might say ours was not a bliss
Were they the ones who got that kiss?

We will continue to celebrate
Until the Warden flies the gate!

Then in your arms, I will rest my head
With no desire to leave our bed

MISSING YOU

I miss your kisses, your gentle touch
Making love with you, I miss so much
Conjugal visits are not the same,
But they sure keep me from going insane

FOR THE GOOD TIMES

The neighbors have not stopped gossiping about me
It's like the family caught a deadly disease

The dealer came to pick up the Benz
I gave him the keys without defense

I have scaled back on my spending sprees
I now realize money doesn't grow on trees

I still think the Feds are watching me
Strange cars, misplaced faces on the block I see

Twenty-five to life has created a strife
You treated me right, so I will remain your wife

FATHER'S DAY

Your physical presence is not a must
Your early release, in God I trust

Your care and love prior to this cruel separation
On this special day has gotten my attention

Happy Father's Day!

STAYING IN TOUCH

I know you must think about the family a lot
Being imprisoned seems like a very big plot

Everyone is doing fine
Your uncle's food is still cheap wine

Graduation time is drawing near
It's the worst of all the dates I fear

Your brother has finally found himself work
Looking no more like the block's only jerk

Your street pharmacist friends are looking swell
The guys in blue are still giving them hell

Mom and Dad are hanging tight
Grandma looks like she is losing the fight

Don't be upset when your collect calls we reject
It's the ridiculous cost of those calls we object

Some of us will visit and some will write
With your family on your side, you must win the fight

WE TRIED ALL WE COULD

I re-tried your case a thousand times
Focused mostly on the prosecutor's lines

Our family portraits I use as the jury
Our entire household is in a fury

How could they not see the truth?
That young DA was a tireless brute!!

The appeals process was put in place
But good heavens, you were in the wrong place

Ballistics, logistics, hard evidence and all…
With the best legal team you took a great fall

BIRTH OF A CHILD

I wish you were in the delivery room
To see our baby exit my womb
For every contraction
I could feel your compassion

Knowing you wanted so much
To see, to hear, to feel and touch
My every move, my every groan
You did not want me to do it alone

HAPPY BIRTHDAY MOTHER

Do not lament the wasted, locked up years
God might have given you enough to spare

Let us celebrate this special day
With hope, love, joy and tears!

HOLD ON TO GOD'S GRACE

Don't spend your days crying
Or seeking the comfort of a friend
Bring your attention directly to God
Because on him, you can depend

LOYALTY

Do not for one moment try to believe
That with each visit I am there to deceive

I'm seeing no one and no one's seeing me
After being with you, who could there be?

NEED OF A FRIEND

Friends and family may turn from you
God is one who will always come through

He doesn't care if you are guilty or not
Do you need a better friend than that?

MERRY CHRISTMAS FATHER

Christmas this year, will bring me no cheer
Simply because you are not here

The star that I will place at the top of the tree
For me will be a symbol that you'll soon be set free

I'll purchase gifts from you to me
And arrange them nicely for all to see

MERRY CHRISTMAS MOTHER

Mom, it's Christmas again
How we wonder how long it has been
For every moment that we are awake
We deeply regret your huge mistake

Your gift is nicely tucked away
As we await that loud hooray
Christmas lights? ... No, not this year!!!
My Mom's absence is too hard too bear

HAPPY BIRTHDAY FATHER

Do not lament the wasted, locked up years
God might have given you enough to spare

Let us celebrate this special day
With hope, love, joy and tears!

REMEMBERING THE GOOD TIMES

I know it must be difficult for you
To stop thinking about the things we used to do

Take all the comfort in knowing this
Our lives together is an eternal bliss
We were prepared to wait as long as it takes
For you to spend the time for your mistakes

The life we shared before your incarceration
For many other families is mere imagination

While you were here, we did it all
So much we shared that I can hardly recall

You might not see or hear from me often
But never for a moment, believe you are forgotten

FRIENDS FOR LIFE

This decision was painstaking for me
Simply asking you to set me free

To stay committed is a senseless thought
This is a tough decision with which I have fought

We must be realistic when you look at our lives
Which in our position, looks like
a formal dinner without knives

I don't mind keeping our friendship the same
But to say I'll wait, is simply insane

Don't try your tactic of scaring me
If you are reasonable in thought, the logic you'll see

I have pledged my support
until your sentence you commute
Giving you no grounds, for my loyalty to dispute

KEEP YOUR HEAD UP

Give up the thoughts that breed discontent
Accept where you are because the rules you bent

Right there behind those iron gates
To bless you bountifully, God awaits

ENCOURAGEMENT

Don't start your day saying how could I?
Just stay focused on getting by

Get rid of the misery of being locked down
Wear your smile and not a frown

Muster the courage to face each day
Your choice is limited – you have no other way

Humble yourself and obey the Guards
Because even in prison there are rewards

HANG TIGHT

Your burden is not too heavy
To be lightened by a daily prayer
No trials or tribulations are too great to bear.

WEDDING ANNIVERSARY

To celebrate another year
Without you being physically here
Makes me feel I should be there
To share your burden and your pain

Honey, I ask of you to simply reflect
On just how beautiful we looked
On that special day, your tux my dress
And all our guests
We must hold tight and never regress

WE ARE IN THIS TOGETHER

At least during your trial, we saw you everyday
Now that you are sentenced, you are so far away
We are all trying hard to get on with our lives
But the victim's family keeps feeding us bad vibes

It takes a lot of guts to hold our heads high
Our only strategy is just to get by
If we are out here and in so much pain
I am sure there are days when you must feel insane

Never ever for one moment flinch
When you are dazed – yourself you must pinch
Reach deep inside and yell to your soul
Get this body out of this hellhole!

MOTHER'S DAY

Your physical presence is not a must
Your early release, in God I trust

Your care and love prior to this cruel separation
On this special day has gotten my attention

Happy Mother's Day

LOVE FOREVER

Physically, you are locked away
Many thought my eyes would stray

Love like ours is very rare
Without each other, our souls are bare

MISSING YOU

Longing for your tight embrace
Missing the radiance of your face

The journey to visit is not very easy
Most of the Guards act quite sleazy

As hard a task each visit might be
Seeing you monthly is a must for me

THOUGHTS OF FATHER

I know full well justice was not served
Day after day I remain disturbed

Afraid for next Father's Day
Simply because you are locked away

Never you give up hope
Because I am holding my end of your rope

MOTHER PASSED

So you missed mother's funeral
Your only hope is a memorial
Stop feeling guilty
You know she was not healthy

I know she worried a lot about you
But there was diabetes, hypertension
and heart disease too
God only took her ahead of you

Keep on fighting to be released
With that her spirit will be pleased

YOUR DNA WILL SOON SET YOU FREE

They claim the jury was contaminated
With that statement, I was elated
The entire trial itself was like a circus
The intent I am sure was to break us

The Prosecutor was quite dapper
His blood-stained evidence was quite a shocker
Crime scene material can be quite decisive
But DNA results are the most impressive

Thank God for the uniqueness of a DNA strand
The Detectives must bury their heads in the sand!
Free at last, free at last!
In but a short while you'll be free at last!

THE CIRCLE IS BROKEN

The social circles to which we belong
Started coming apart when your trial began

Now that you are sentenced and gone to do time
The phone calls and good wishes are literally mimed

The attitude and support of family and friends will wane
But do not for one moment let that drive you insane

$$ TIME

Embezzlement, fraud with intent to deceive
The media frenzy got all to believe
I never thought it would end this way
For a while your lawyers had them at bay

Time in prison is more boring than sad
You'll miss the luxurious life that you had
The rigging of numbers for monetary gain
Historically drives Judges and Jurors insane!

FINDING HUMOR WHILE DOING TIME

White-collared crime, a term so sublime
I wonder what the author had in mind

A blue-collared worker pinches a little cash
but the white-collared guy hoards a huge stash

Here's hoping that while doing time
for your white-collared crime
You'll take time out to drop me a line

THINK LIFE OVER
WHILE YOU'RE LOCKED AWAY

Since you've been gone I have time to look back
What really had possessed you to start selling crack?

The mere destruction of lives it can cause
Should have been enough to put that idea on pause

You made more enemies than friends on the street
Your entire effort met great feat

Use this time to contemplate
And really analyze your huge mistake

Your family loves you world without end
Endurance, embrace and good wishes we send

ENCOURAGEMENT FOR A PAROLE VIOLATOR

Parole violation is the worst time to serve
You hit the Parole Officer's bad nerve

I know it was difficult to walk a straight line
With the distractions of the world all intertwined

Do not try to keep track of the days
Time locked away can be used in many ways

Just be assured it must come to an end
Strong helping hands I am here to lend

WE LOVE YOU UNCONDITIONALLY

You were tried in the court of public opinion
The condemnation and chastisement were past oblivion

I am in shock you committed such an act
Totally floored by the undisputed fact

Even though we are disappointed in you
Frankly speaking - what can we do?

We'll send letters, care packages
and accept your phone calls
'Cause you'll be pretty lonely behind those gray walls

YOUR INNOCENCE YOU MUST DEFEND TO THE END

It must be painful to be wrongly accused
As an onlooker, I am totally confused

Encouraging you to hang in there
Knowing you are innocent is really not fair

You were uprooted from a structured life
A blatant lie has stirred up great strife

I am not upset with the Jurors or Judge
They were all mislead by the cop's palpable grudge

For a peaceful life I want to say hang tight
But on second thought, you should put up a fight!

We'll pay a lawyer to start your appeal
The truth of this matter, we must reveal

Until this process is put in place
Hold yourself together and pray for God's grace.

THE POLITICS OF PRISON LIFE

Correction facility?

With such rigidity?

That is pure absurdity

The irony of it all
Is that they expect reform behind a wall

YOU WERE UNFAIRLY TREATED

As a first time offender
Your freedom you surrendered

Couldn't they have given you a break?
Considering it was your first mistake

But no...
they have you locked down making license plates
While your life on the outside deteriorates

THE POLITRICKS OF IMPRISONMENT

The prison industrial complex
Has got me perplexed!

The goal of the gatekeeper is to make him some money
So your incarceration, he finds it funny

Frankly speaking, this is no joke
My back is breaking with his heavy yoke!

THE SYSTEM NEEDS MENDING

Minimum mandatory sentencing
Is a term that could use some mending

How can one impose such stiff penalty
When the justice system is so flawed and filthy

There is no proof that serving mandatory sentences
In any way reduces the number of offenses

HEALING

What more can we really do?
The appeals process failed us too

I know that anger you must sometimes feel
But try finding a way and start to heal

GOD IS YOUR JUDGE

Trying to get rid of the Writ of Habeas Corpus
Is technically a way to simply dismiss us

They chip away at our legal tools
All in an effort to keep us as fools

They can exhaust your efforts to get out of jail
It is God who grants us the winning bail

He bails us out of our sinful ways
Leaving the enemy in a daze

DISPENSATION OF JUSTICE, IS IT FOR REAL?

Dispensation of justice is what they like to proclaim
But it's based on a system that is so very lame

Sometimes justice has color
Sometimes justice has height
Sometimes justice for one is another's great plight

Sometimes justice is skewed
With that hatred is brewed

Sometimes justice is bought
Sometimes justice is sold
It is bartered at times like silver and gold

MISSING YOU AT THANKSGIVING

The last Thursday of every November
Should this year simply not be remembered
Reckon being it's Thanksgiving Day
And you are cruelly locked away

Your Auntie's yam
Grandmas's ham

Your uncle's liquor keeps us quite mellow
That grandpa of ours is quite some fellow
Collared greens and the turkey's legs
Are the portions I recall you liked the best

As we sit down to eat this year
We will pretend that you're right here

YOUR CHILDREN MISS YOU

Your absence has truly affected the boys
They have no interest in school – not even their toys

The Guidance Counselor has been very gracious
The Sunday-School teacher has more than helped us

I have come to realize they are truly a mess
When I drive by McDonalds and they are not impressed

Nonetheless they are doing fine
We are all just out here counting time

YOUR DAUGHTER MISSES YOU

The teacher reports she's distracted in class
Sort of like staring into an empty glass

Maybe hoping she'll see your reflection
Your absence then would be a deception

THE KIDS AND I MISS YOU A LOT

The kids miss you a lot!
That's an undisputed fact

Our son has started acting wild
He's not the usual well-behaved child

We spend a lot of quality time together
I am now the parent to whom they are tethered

At nights they climb into our bed
To rest their little sleepy head

MISSING OUT ON FAMILY TIME

The baby busted his first tooth
Everyone thinks he looks so cute

I know you wanted to see him grow
But unfortunately you were dealt with a big blow

I'll take him to see you when he's old enough
At this stage of the game it could be a little too much

You can rely on me to do the best I can
'Cause prior to this, our family we had planned

Even though I cannot take your place
Trust me darling I am in control of the base

KEEPING IN TOUCH

Never thought you'd be in one place
This penal system has you running a race
I write to you here, I hear you're gone there
I write to you there, they say you are on your way here

Guys are shuttled from jail to jail
Missing out on their families comforting mail
What's the logic of moving from prison A to B?
There is never anything new in a jail for one to see!

Trust you'll remain here for the rest of your term
Staying in one place helps one to stand firm

GET OUT ALIVE

They say you are there for rehabilitation
That to me, is mere humiliation

You and I know full well
Prison is the epitome of hell

Do your very best to survive
You must get out of there alive!

YOUR FAMILY'S THOUGHTS

You committed a crime that was so very bad
It has made the entire family sad
We are seriously thinking to relocate
Staying around here makes us suffocate

We feel a great sense of loss on your part
But you have broken the victim's families' heart
Even grandma in her senile state
In her lucid moments, gets so irate

We are here to say your blood runs through our vein
On that particular day you must have gone insane
For the family of the victim we show our love
Truly endorsed by the God up above

THINK ON THESE THINGS...

No fighting of wars
No screeching cars

No blazing guns
No sidewalk garbage and lazy bums

No need to worry about terror alert
You guys are the safest population on earth

I am here trying to make sense of it all
Helping you cope with life behind that great wall

Here's trying to find logic in your incarceration
As you can see I have poor imagination

DON'T BE DISMAYED

Your punishment doesn't fit your crime
Folks have done worse and gotten less time

But the justice system is the most flawed in this town
From top to bottom, they are a bunch of clowns

The jokers dealt you a very bad deck
Just say to yourself what the heck?

Walk a straight line and make no mistakes
In no time the Warden will announce your release date

Don't harbor thoughts of trying to escape
On that glorious day, just head for the gate!

HAPPY VALENTINE'S DAY
TO MY LOVE DOING TIME

Even though you are locked away
I still wish you a Happy Valentine's Day

Your love I am and will always be
Your beautiful face I can't wait to see

Your romantic lines, and enchanting eyes
Always on this day brings me good vibes

Happy Valentine's Day

KEEPING YOU HAPPY

I'll send funds to your commissary
Keeping you happy is very necessary

I know you as a guy who was always well maintained
Slightly bordering on being vain

I might not visit as often as I should
But I'm sure you know I would if I could

NEEDLESS PUNISHMENT

Imprisonment is really a brutal punishment
It seems like transgressing a social sacrament

They have taken you from your family and friends
Hypocritically suggesting that your life you'll mend

I strongly protest this senseless move
You don't have to be imprisoned for your life to improve

CHANGE YOUR POSTURE
WHILE YOU'RE DOING TIME

There are things in life that can help you stay the same
I suggest at this point you switch your lane

And there are things in life that can help you change
Please choose those and control your rage

I encourage you to use this time to focus on
Those things that will change your life

CELL BLOCK LIFE

Cell-block life
With all its strife
Watch your back he might have a knife!!

A call to the yard for recreation time
Get dressed quickly and get on the line

I know you're not used to having your movements ordered
Just comply with the rules you might just be rewarded

TAKE HEED

I'm sure you're tired of hearing me say
The company you keep can lead you astray
You placed yourself in a precarious position
I'm sure you now know that was a wrong decision

Flashy cars and expensive clothes
Did you really need them? God only knows
When you come home you must start anew
Your friends I'm sure will be very few

TIME IN THE SERVICE NOW TIME BEHIND BARS

You came back home disillusioned by the war
Since that time your thoughts been afar

They lured you into their military
Now you find yourself in solitary

The system brought you to this place
It's a well known fact they target your race

Physically you might be in jail
Your spirit and mind have long exhaled

PLAYING IT SAFE AND STAYING ALIVE

Weapons posession
Coerced confessions

Unlawful searches
Leads to skirmishes

Drug paraphernalia
Ethnic paranoia

Reaching for a wallet
Could put you in a casket

Don't disobey cops
They'll bust your chops

Rules you break puts you in jail
Rules others break was simply a mistake

We're all on life's court playing life's game
But as you have discovered the rules are not the same